THE WOVEN FLAG

THE WOVEN FLAG

MARGARET FOURT GOKA

BookVenture Publishing LLC
1000 Country Lane Ste 300
Ishpeming MI 49849
www.bookventure.com
Hotline: 1(877) 276-9751
Fax: 1(877) 864-1686

Ordering Information:
Quantity sales. Special discounts are available on quantity purchases by corporations, associations, and others. For details, contact the publisher at the address above.

Printed in the United States of America

ISBN-13: Softcover   978-1-946492-70-8
          Pdf   978-1-946492-71-5
          ePub   978-1-946492-72-2
          Kindle   978-1-946492-73-9

Rev. date: 02/23/2017

For Lyman
There's a loom in New York that can weave the American flag.
From an anecdote

Sunnyvale, California
2012

CONTENTS

III. PLACES

IV. RIDDLES

V. CAFFEINE AND WINE

VI. FAMILY

ELEMENT

Willow wants water
Wind breathes song
Chill flees fire
Earth urges each sense.

Twig takes light
Root thirsts
Warmth opens bud
Leaf lies on earth again.

Dirt, wet, air, and heat
Are elemental threads
And web all life,
Strands to catch a design.

I. HOME

FOR CHILDREN

I wove three little flags,
A one, a two, and a three,
And one Appalachian flag,
And one Yonkers flag,
and three little flags
flew at my house.

Not only flew
(A one, a two, a three),
but spoke
and said

Give me apple, give me pear
Give me extra 'tato chip to feed to my friend the bear.

Katey Corn grew in a field of Kansas light,
while Betsy Noodle curled to sleep.
Bird lit on the corn.
Noodle woke up and grew.

Oh baby!
A one, a two and a THREE!

A CHILD

You fuse nations and races.
You span cultures, oceans,
a union of east and west.
You have in you dark and light,
male and female, strong and delicate.
Will you be able to wiggle your nose?
You are my invasion,
his victory, our offspring.

BABY IN APRIL

For Katie

Time goes lightly,
I watch you while
small leaves start.
Your needs alternate
to cling or free yourself.
The sun blesses small startings;
I am patient, sitting while you
and the leaves both come out
and return. A light day
rests in the air.

KATE

You have a quiet center
even now. A contented kitten
you wrap up with body and limbs.

As you grow we will see
more of the center.
You will be poised on the outside.
That center will show.

Now keep it inside
like a toy in your pocket,
a story in your desk.

Childhood is a spaceship full of friends
that rockets into the future.
I will be there when it lands
like a kitten on its feet,
and your bright face and dark hair
will lead me to let you be
the young woman.

The seed in your center is a plum pit.
Now the branch bides. I know
the sun will bring out the twig and the leaf
and the young person.

MORNING

Bird voices celebrate morning,
Water boils. Child sleeps
and husband and cat pursue
their business outside.
The crimson flower blooms.

MUSING

When the light is gone
We seek ourselves
Musing
Emptying our minds like the plum.
The fruit was crashing all afternoon.

Snail syntax: silver footsteps' curly journeys;
They bit the fruit
That morning finds fallen.
The snails' ways lead erratically.

We wait to eat up to the seed
Of sleep in the delicious dark.
Summer is gentle here. Will the baby
Let me dream?

THIS EVENING

Some of the toys are right side up
And some are the other way round.
A shelf holds children's books piled sideways
The floor is full, the bottom shelves half empty.
This disorderly corner is the heart of the house.
We escape, staring at the television
Or open a chest full of toys and take them all out.

One daughter sleeps and the smaller one
Finally tires and goes to bed.
Whose bed? Mine!
Only deep in sleep can she be transferred to her crib.

It is a happy quiet that finally comes late to the house.
Two chatterboxes sleep.
Winter is mild and we stay well
Two dolls and a teddy bear sleep on the rug.

CHRISTMAS POEM

As I cleared the table, I listened to the plates.
I moved the cups.
I heard the forks and spoons ting
And I heard the scrape of the empty kettle
As I settled the clean pot upside down, drying.

It was too noisy:
Clowns jumped in the television,
Cars roared,
An airplane pressed its thumbs over my ears,
So I sent the dog outside.

The water ran.
The children washed and brushed and dried their hair.
The dark deepened.
The water stopped running.
Husband lit his pipe.

I went outside.
The fence was quiet.
The houses were quiet. So was the dog.
Before we got cold we listened together.

Listen, listen for Christmas.
Find the sound of sharing
And the talk of gathering.
Look in the light at the words of celebration.

Listen to evergreens and sidewalks
And people carrying packages.
Listen to the maple leaf buds waiting for spring.
Hear the clouds storming,
Then hear them walk away.

The kettle is quiet when you set it aside.
So are the cups and the bowls.
Wait and hear a wish.
Will you say Noel? Noel.

ODE TO SCHOOL

I sort the wash,
A mothercooklaundress, never
A poet, oh no,
A grunge, a cinder maiden. Oh me!

I sing at my work if
The children and their rhymes times time
Voices go off down the walk,
Hopping over the stones and bushes
To school.

ROBBIE'S POEM

Robin, I haven't stepped back yet
And written a poem for you.
New girl, on her feet,
Voicing her feelings everywhere,
Singing out, trying everything,
Learning the shape of life,
Testing the world.

Independent, flying free,
Flying back.
You say, "Up"
And when I pick you up
There are hugs and kisses.
No, I can't be sad long near you.

Birdie, the nest is complete with you in it.
I can wait for spring because delight
Sings in my daughter's easy laughter.

A REPORT TO THE BOARD

I. The Rehearsal

Dancing up the stair step
To the front

The children spun a golden trail
From bales of straw.

Rumple, rumple Stiltsken.

II. The Pageant

Rumple, rumple bump
Plod the camels and the shepherds
Rumple bump!
The star fell down.

Close the curtain and let the imagination
Wend back to the tale.

The tale of the family,
The poor family
Yearning for cabbage
Growing in someone else's field,
Needing a place to stay for deliverance,
Wanting a livelihood.

Legends to spin, tales to recite
Lessons to play.

FRUIT FLIES AND AN OMEN

The fruit is in,
and sunlight blasts the back yard.
Hello roof, my house looks
bald without the fig branching
over the roof.
Everyone's been piling their green fruit
by the curb.
Everyone's been fighting fruit flies.

We give up our fruit
and endure the wash of poison from helicopters.
The fruit is in, torn off
aborted, violated.
downed.
Great bones of branch lie about in piles.

I am sure it will leaf out again
next spring, somehow.
But I am unsure
unsettled, as if I were unhoused.

Have I been mourning again?
When will I come home to myself?

AT KAY'S

Play dough on the patio,
animal crackers in the kitchen,
the peaceful sun in the garden
lights Sunday morning.

Hummingbirds chase each other
and a huge dragonfly lands,
looks at us in the sandbox,
and leaves.

The hills are bright and quiet
Except for the chickens next door.
Soon it will be time to leave all this.
Will we regret such friendly light days?

BONDING

Tact is feeling.
Feeling is the central sense for me.
I have no vista.
My sights comb the rug for crayons that the baby could swallow.
Hearing? I miss pieces of everything I am told.
I hear cries.
I don't hear each crisp separate word.
I gobble, so that takes care of taste.
Smell, my nose does work.
I love the smells of the laundry when it's clean
Of the baby's neck, of her Ivory Snow clothes:
I hate the smell of ammonia.
Feeling, a certain weight in my arms,
A need, when my breasts are too full.
Bonding is touching, holding, parenting, enabling life to unfold.

II. ANIMALS

WORDS FOR CHILDREN

The cat understands
Under stairs,
Under boxes, under chairs.

The cat has an intuition
For the insides of bags
And the fluttering of rags.

The cat takes a twitch
For a ghost or a witch,
And will jump on a lump
If it smiles.

WIND SIGHT

Golden cat
You are the golden cat
You are a song
To the goddess

There you sit, a shadow
Before my glass door, kept
In a person's house
Listening to birds,

Capable of kittens
And great wars with rodents,
Capable of song and purr and *mrr*

You are the golden cat
Inside a lattice work of black
Like prison bars holding the spirit of life
Away from the world.

DEPARTURE

Cat spirit leaving
She twitched the end of her tail
Passively waiting,
Then stopped.

Ill for months, thinner and thinner,
Coaxed to eat
She lost her appetite for life.

Always affectionate,
Content indoors,
She would venture to the garden
A few feet from the door to sleep
Or lie in the catnip.

I will miss her,
But her spirit is set free.

Where spirits go
She will twitch her whole tail
And purr.

WHAT IF?

There is a kind of cow made of dappled light in the back yard.
She munches on the meager grass in the morning,
and stands in my orchard with blossoms near her eyes.
At night, at evening, my pasture's cow slowly goes
to wander among the stars until she comes out of
that great domed barn of hers to see the first light
and munch all day.

SUMMER WISH

If I were a hummingbird
I would live on insects and nectar.
I would follow the blooming of flowers
and leave when the flowers were spent.
I would hum and hover
an aerial acrobat
scooping flying bugs into my long beak,
and with my even longer tongue, sipping
the sweetness inside flowers.

I would live free of the constraints of
being human.
To fly like that I'd spend my days
visiting flowers, cooling down to near hibernation at night,
warming up when the sun returns,
and always flying where the world blooms.

III. PLACES

SONG

My home, my life
My house, my dreams

O sum be something

My song, my breath,
My house, my dreams

O song, be something

Home of my song, my house
Body of my dreams, my home

Wreath of dry sticks
Cannot frame my sight

Yet song of my home hums,
Yet does a road lead out

The meadow gone to orchard
The orchards to housing

Snow drifts from the cherry flowers
Rain follows, soaks, inundates

Drums, drums on the roof all day.

COOK'S CANYON

1. The Upper Dam

Water is still to the bottom, dark in shade
Until I toss one thumbnail-big pebble and
Scare a frog to ripple the pine and locust
Reflected on the black perfect pool.
The marred surface radiates circles
Until the pebble settles, the frog sinks below.

A web breathes in the gentle air.
How long have I been dreaming?
The near road forgotten, all the going forgotten,
And Sound is a transparent dark depth
Opening within like the gut twang of a frog.

2. The Lower Dam

A dragonfly flits in the sunlight.
Fish know the roots of lily pads
Like quiet priests submerged in knowledge.
A fine dust of gnats blows out skimming the surface.
A bird flies in the reflected sky.

IN THE CITY OF THE BROKEN FURNACE

In the city of the broken furnace
there is a block of Victoriana tenements
sixty years old and older, standing
the weather, and of course, the smoke,
shaking with the traffic passing, and
sometimes smoldering
with the current wired through
their plaster and insect ridden wood.

At the edge of this city
stood an apartment, owned
by all the usual crooks.
Three girl students, we paid our rent.
Dead into January after exams,
the place was up for sale,
so no one would fix the heat.

Cold like that on the third floor
one remembers in terms of friends
whose kindness one had to bargain for,
whose warmth one gently accepts.

Never again may we have to live
in the city of broken furnaces,
cinders, and sulfurous red smog.

MEMORY OF OLIN LIBRARY

God knows it's cold
On the third floor
When your furnace is broken.

We lived in the library
In January
Or visited friends.
Keeping the oven on didn't help much
Wearing sweaters was not enough.

The library was heaven.
I spent so much time there
You could have delivered
The mail to me on the fifth floor.

I lived there with
Paper dust books tables other carrels
And shelves,
When I didn't have to eat,
Sleep or go to class.

EDENS

This is Eden, this fig
Thrust above the ground
with huge leaves, a battleground of squirrels.
Earth did not know woman
at first.

Yet here I drink tea
picked with labor, purchased, sent
from far outside this fence
of hewn hammered boards,
keeping Eden in. Does it exist?

We say Eden, remembering
but not knowing where,
culture's memory of a place without woman
Or work. Instead of knowledge, innocence.

Creation recreates itself. Figs grow.
The natural world continues
shaped by natural laws.
whether we work on it or not,
Eden reasserts itself
to heal the scars our work and plunder
leave upon the earth.

Squirrels fuss in the fig.
Somewhere a woman is paid for her work
picking tea. Adam cannot slumber.
The laws of the sun touch through the shade
and write on the ground. It is fall.

POEM FOR A SMALL PAGE

Steam from the cauliflower
Quietly rises;
The dinner cooks.
The timer ticks.
Life isn't endless
But green persists
In the backyard
The grass hanging on
Through the drought.

IV. RIDDLES

THE THIEF

Oh wild world, beset by comets
And nuclear arms and
Fires burning beyond our imagination,
Despite this terrible universe,
We can come home to the stars and the hillside
So much more easily than
We can come home to our fellows, our families, and our friends.

UNMATCHED DUALITY

It's there, it begins, it has
Fat and strident tension,
It has concavity like a hammock,
It has a rope snaking.
At 2:00 it has a sheath.

Otherwise it's still there, and
It begins Johnny Walker smooth,
It has, puzzlingly,
A piece of marshmallow.
I recall how damn scared I was,
I stop, I go on,
And it has ended.

ENTER

1. *into the world- a runner*

The chariot tips over
and spills light everywhere.
I speed into the day,
spending every breath upon movement
with never a glance down for
the world that my spinning feet turn.

2. *into the dream- a sleeper*

Quick in the sun, the sky's spider casts
a spun shadow and I drop my hands,
my fingers shapeless.
The cup shatters, the world slips,
and a sleeper topples
through a drifted web.

3. *into the poem- a dreamer*

I am balancing the
globe upon my palm,
the shape complete and alight.
The dream comes out of sleep whole.
A universe creates within me
as I wake.

HOMESPUN

What is homespun?
Cloak of gray, gray woolen dress, stockings
But all we have are colors,
Spun rocks, spun plastics, spun paper,
Or cottons
Wrinkling and soaked in sweat.
Why do I want a linen apron
Over a homespun skirt?

I spin the wash, twisting the family's colors
Shaking them out carefully
Folding them up,
And hastily putting them away.
What is homespun?

What do I owe?
Could I sell rabbit angora, carrots, apricots
Strawberries, figs
And sweet gum balls dressed as Christmas stars?
Make pine needle pillows stitched from our rags?
Sell outgrown toys and records?
Am I worth what I owe?

RIDDLES

Only if water flows without
buoying me, can I drown.

*

If the world were a lamp
and a home
only my own tears could blur me.

*

Nothing is to be found
without waiting.

*

I would be found
continually, as the sun finds the world
each morning.

*

What is my depth? Sound me.

*

The flow is between each heartbeat.

*

The light is within me as I grow.

*

I will not be alone when I am caught
by breathlessness.

*

Poetry waits to be written by an inkless pen
upon a page whose clean blank will remain
unmarked.

*

Which is eternal, Life or Death?
To be free is to be indivisible.

*

Books and music reach you when you reach a vision of yourself
and your universe.
The inner universe reflects the outer universe.
No guide takes you anywhere but within.

THE ROSE

The rose is cradled between
Leaves of fern and willow
Opening its bud between
Sides of a vase and two candles.

My table which is set
With this bouquet and light
And rainbow cloth
Is where I work, my desk.
If needed, it is my family table.

Beyond my notebook is Mexico,
And the stark winter forest
Of Maryland. Owls and a little girl
Walking in her kimono
Are closer; men fishing the deep
Pacific are farther away.

To be silly, one hen sits
On a checkered nest near
Maryland, and varied leaves
Fill in the background.

I write what I see
Like a sketch, but come back
To the rose opening
Before my eyes.

MORE MORNINGS

News of turmoil, traffic obsessively
stirs in the lethargy after dawn.
I don't make wishes for pure calm.

I regret there are no trees near our windows.
It reassures the dreaming spirit
like recognizing the Presence, to hear
birds close by in the restless waiting
for the dawn of a mechanical day.

LIGHT'S BALANCE

Yesterday was the Equinox.
I felt the evening's balance
With the day
And dread and memory of cold and dark
Crossed my thoughts, but I dwelt
On the present need to
Buy more oak to burn.

The other day an ironwood log
Burned for two days from
Ember to ash to nearly nothing.
Such solidity slowly reduced
By fire and time.

We'll draw together and solve love's equation.
In March, light will again balance with dark.
Had winter's love come in summer,
Let summer's love bum red in fall.
Why haven't we celebrated the Equinox yet?

TO COMFORT A WOMAN
WHO HAS LOST A CHILD

Remember your child is taken care of
Always by loving hands
Then, now;
I don't know about forever.
Does anyone?

The cuddly baby, the exploring child,
the story teller, guessing, learning
coming of age, the adolescent
hopeful and diligent.

Whenever your child was taken away from you,
Torn in a way,
There is mending to do.
So mend. Scar over it.
Get up and put down your grief.

Maybe you keep a little pocket
handkerchief of grief
but you go on.

THE RUINED TEMPLE

My temple is in ruins.
Still, it is there,
Not where I live,
Where I come to.

I go there in my mind and see the stones in disarray.
I am too old to lift up those fallen stones.
I sit on one to empty my mind, to find room for the present.
The past lies around me like fallen statuary and carvings.

Stand up. Leave the temple of the past.
Deal with the present.
Leave the holy calm of sleep.

V. CAFFEINE AND WINE

JANIGRO'S CONCERT

The cello speaks a language
Other than English.
The thermostat's at 69.
Outside the sun is obvious, triumphant and yells
"Blue Sky Cafe."
I'm into Lipton's tea with milk.
Talk to me while I wash the dishes
And listen to the thermostat's
Dialogue with the heater.
In the furnace a coal
Reduces and reduces to a red glow.
Infinity is the comfort of life
And the pain of trying to speak languages
You have not made your own.

COFFEE

Coffee tastes
Like ground up books
And
Swallowed philosophies
Eliminated
Later.

LENTEN POEM

Green tea on Sunday afternoons tastes like earth and summer
In spring. I want to hatch words. While Easter's in the offing,
The words lay unspoken, unwritten, hard boiling in my brain.

I read fine words and funny words; I kitten to my pilot; I dream.
You want to know why I don't write letters and don't type poems.
Sun banishes the fog and days are either clear or drenched.
I work at worry, the distant men wolves cry, cars swish, swish.

One year, traffic will seem quiet, and I may find in my ragged perceptions
only my kitchen table.
Old and wise, I shall hope to find paper and pen
And due to a fine full pot of tea,
To write realms.

DROUGHT

I'm at the end of my patience,
I'm at the end of my rope.

I'm at the end of summer,
The end of fall
The middle
Of Indian summer
The end of green.

I thirst, I dry up
I am gold, brown, gray

Waiting for silver rain,
Mist, fog,
Waiting for a shawl of water evaporating
From the warm fence,
Warm loam, warm land.

I am waiting to transform
Into gentle winter rain.

VI. Family

FAMILY STONES

Life is a pot full of tea,
a vase of chrysanthemums
lasting longer than the wake.
Life is cupping water in hands,
or swimming across the river to see wild iris.
Life is Obon and Hallowe'en, the dead
leaving their graves, or returning
in August to visit the living.

Life is watering and pulling weeds
from the stones that mark our memories
of the dead.

SUN SADNESS

You know, I miss you now.
I'm homesick. This arid land
We water half the year
Has no home like yours.
The bricks stand in my mind

And remain in place.
Here the sun shines on the fruit leaves.
I would wrap myself in a druid's meditative robes
And worship deciduous forests on my plateau.

Maple and oak and sweetgum, mulberry,
apple, beech enchant me with remembered diversity.
I am sad in the sun wishing for a forest
to wander the long day through.

LOST SINGING

Through the kitchen windows, here's the mourning dove.
Late in the afternoon I'm alone with the kitchen and the dove.
Often I see it outside, but it seldom speaks.
Now the gentle coo links me to deciduous hills of childhood.
So seldom I am alone to pause and listen.

Poetry feeds on solitude and pining like that call.
Doves have grown quiet and lost their liquid song,
Keeping secret the simple message that could mark one's home
with sad content.

Dove, be with us, and remember to sing.

CLOTH

We are made of fibers
like catgut, for violins,
catgut which purrs on the tennis court,
or sings out in concerts.

Our mental fibers are plaid with memory,
old fields and borders of trees,
selvages of river, beaches,
ribbons of roads.
Where we've been.

Fiber wears and wears out.
We are elastic. We return to shape.
Our health mends.
Our hearts guide us like the principle
which sends the shuttle through the loom
weaving, relentless but purposeful.

Fiber lasts also.
After the seam is gone
and the color faded, grayed,
and the texture become soft and fuzzy with age,
after all that wear the weave may last.

Scraps. Made of fibers, we
will become in time scraps,
disassociated pieces, unquilted.
In time the plaid of time is lost.
The scraps of weaving remain a while longer.

Ask the wind about the dust.
What process unravels our fibers?
How were we twisted and spun and wound and formed?
We almost know, though we don't know why.

AUNT MARY'S SOIREE

I was going to sleep
And really practically was asleep
When I heard
Aunt Mary come over to my house
With two friends.
The three of them talked
Laughed, and decided
Not to wake me up.
Two men, and Aunt Mary,
Like old times when
The couch facing the fireplace
Wore denim covers all winter.
So, when I told dear,
He said, "Are you sure
You heard Aunt Mary come over, and talk?"
"So, maybe," I said, "I was dreaming."
"I think you *were* dreaming," he said.

CHILD OF SMOKE

From the time when I was small she was
inside her blue cloud
when I went to find her.

Bitter at the edge
her smoke was between us.
I accepted that I would find her
a little out of reach.

But I came to tell and ask
or look at her as she thought
across the dining room table from me
in front of the windows to the back yard.

Her immediate surroundings were ephemeral.
I could reach through them
but before I was sure of this
I would squawk to get attention.

Since my life separated from hers,
I see her again waiting to be interrupted
in her place, smoking.

FAMILIARITIES

Knowing I am loved, I can love.
I will bear children
And put them to my breast.
You must make a garden for us,
And see that a roof is raised
Over our heads. I will keep
The floor smooth and peel the potatoes.
The children shout and race about,
Swing and climb, sleep, and nibble.
We keep a sphinx who understands all this.
Don't you be a riddle, too.
I say I love you,
And knowing you are loved, now
Can you say, you love me?

HEART WORK

I am very still
Looking for a spring, a gear,
a meshing together that is apart
Unable to mend until
I find the rent, the rip, the tear.
Concentrated beyond listening
I wait for the light to get strong
To search for my flaw.
Why do I hope I could be perfect?
Mother, if only you'd speak to me
That would not be radio *gaga*.

CPSIA information can be obtained
at www.ICGtesting.com
Printed in the USA
FFOW02n1153281217
44173494-43574FF